# The Key Facts™ on Qatar

I0469056

*Essential Information on Qatar*

By Patrick W. Nee

The Internationalist®
www.internationalist.com

**The Internationalist**®

*International Business, Investment, and Travel*

**Published by:**

The Internationalist Publishing Company

96 Walter Street/ Suite 200

Boston, MA 02131, USA

Tel: 617-354-7722

www.internationalist.com

PN@internationalist.com

# *Table Of Contents*

Chapter 1: Background

Chapter 2: Geography

Chapter 3: People and Society

Chapter 4: Government

Chapter 5: Economy

Chapter 6: Energy

Chapter 7: Communications

Chapter 8: Transportation

Chapter 9: Military

# Chapter 1: Background

Ruled by the Al Thani family since the mid-1800s, Qatar transformed itself from a poor British protectorate noted mainly for pearling into an independent state with significant oil and natural gas revenues. During the late 1980s and early 1990s, the Qatari economy was crippled by a continuous siphoning off of petroleum revenues by the Amir, who had ruled the country since 1972. His son, the current Amir HAMAD bin Khalifa Al Thani, overthrew him in a bloodless coup in 1995. In 2001, Qatar resolved its longstanding border disputes with both Bahrain and Saudi Arabia. As of 2007, oil and natural gas revenues had enabled Qatar to attain the highest per capita income in the world. Qatar has not experienced the level of unrest or violence seen in other Near Eastern and North African countries in 2010-11, due in part to its immense wealth. Qatar's international image is bolstered in part by the Doha-based Al Jazirah news network, which has provided comprehensive coverage of the Near East and North African Arab revolutions. Additionally, Qatar played a significant role in the Libyan revolution by pressing the Gulf Cooperation Council and the Arab League to assist the Libyan rebel movement.

# Chapter 2: Geography

**Location:**

Middle East, peninsula bordering the Persian Gulf and Saudi Arabia

**Geographic coordinates:**

25 30 N, 51 15 E

**Map references:**

Middle East

**Area:**

total: 11,586 sq km

country comparison to the world: 166

land: 11,586 sq km

water: 0 sq km

**Area - comparative:**

slightly smaller than Connecticut

**Land boundaries:**

total: 60 km

border countries: Saudi Arabia 60 km

**Coastline:**

563 km

**Maritime claims:**

territorial sea: 12 nm

contiguous zone: 24 nm

exclusive economic zone: as determined by bilateral agreements or the median line

**Climate:**

arid; mild, pleasant winters; very hot, humid summers

**Terrain:**

    mostly flat and barren desert covered with loose sand and gravel

**Elevation extremes:**

    lowest point: Persian Gulf 0 m

    highest point: Tuwayyir al Hamir 103 m

**Natural resources:**

    petroleum, natural gas, fish

**Land use:**

    arable land: 1.64%

    permanent crops: 0.27%

    other: 98.09% (2005)

**Irrigated land:**

    130 sq km (2002)

**Total renewable water resources:**

    0.1 cu km (1997)

**Freshwater withdrawal (domestic/industrial/agricultural):**

    total: 0.29 cu km/yr (24%/3%/72%)

    per capita: 358 cu m/yr (2000)

**Natural hazards:**

    haze, dust storms, sandstorms common

**Environment - current issues:**

    limited natural freshwater resources are increasing dependence on large-scale desalination facilities

**Environment - international agreements:**

    party to: Biodiversity, Climate Change, Climate Change-Kyoto Protocol, Desertification, Endangered Species, Hazardous Wastes, Law of the Sea, Ozone Layer Protection, Ship Pollution

    signed, but not ratified: none of the selected agreements

**Geography - note:**

strategic location in central Persian Gulf near major petroleum deposits

# Chapter 3: People and Society

**Nationality:**

noun: Qatari(s)

adjective: Qatari

**Ethnic groups:**

Arab 40%, Indian 18%, Pakistani 18%, Iranian 10%, other 14%

**Languages:**

Arabic (official), English commonly used as a second language

**Religions:**

Muslim 77.5%, Christian 8.5%, other 14% (2004 census)

**Population:**

1,951,591 (July 2012 est.)

country comparison to the world: 147

**Age structure:**

0-14 years: 12.5% (male 124,303/female 120,568)

15-24 years: 14.4% (male 207,942/female 73,555)

25-54 years: 68.9% (male 1,105,087/female 240,000)

55-64 years: 3.3% (male 49,965/female 14,668)

65 years and over: 0.8% (male 9,312/female 6,191) (2012 est.)

**Median age:**

total: 32.2 years

male: 33.2 years

female: 27.8 years (2012 est.)

**Population growth rate:**

4.93% (2012 est.)

country comparison to the world: 1

**Birth rate:**

10.23 births/1,000 population (2012 est.)

country comparison to the world: 191

**Death rate:**

1.55 deaths/1,000 population (July 2012 est.)

country comparison to the world: 224

**Net migration rate:**

40.62 migrant(s)/1,000 population (2012 est.)

country comparison to the world: 1

**Urbanization:**

urban population: 96% of total population (2010)

rate of urbanization: 1.6% annual rate of change (2010-15 est.)

**Major cities - population:**

DOHA (capital) 427,000 (2009)

**Sex ratio:**

at birth: 1.02 male(s)/female

under 15 years: 1.03 male(s)/female

15-64 years: 4.15 male(s)/female

65 years and over: 1.5 male(s)/female

total population: 3.29 male(s)/female (2011 est.)

**Maternal mortality rate:**

7 deaths/100,000 live births (2010)

country comparison to the world: 167

**Infant mortality rate:**

total: 6.81 deaths/1,000 live births

country comparison to the world: 164

male: 7.08 deaths/1,000 live births

female: 6.53 deaths/1,000 live births (2012 est.)

**Life expectancy at birth:**

total population: 78.09 years

country comparison to the world: 55

male: 76.11 years

female: 80.12 years (2012 est.)

**Total fertility rate:**

1.93 children born/woman (2012 est.)

country comparison to the world: 137

**Health expenditures:**

2.5% of GDP (2009)

country comparison to the world: 183

**Physicians density:**

2.757 physicians/1,000 population (2006)

**Hospital bed density:**

1.4 beds/1,000 population (2008)

**Sanitation facility access:**

improved:

*urban*: 100% of population

*rural*: 100% of population

*total*: 100% of population

**HIV/AIDS - adult prevalence rate:**

less than 0.1% (2009 est.)

country comparison to the world: 149

**HIV/AIDS - people living with HIV/AIDS:**

fewer than 200 (2009 est.)

country comparison to the world: 159

**HIV/AIDS - deaths:**

fewer than 100 (2009 est.)

country comparison to the world: 128

**Education expenditures:**

    3.3% of GDP (2005)

    country comparison to the world: 121

**Literacy:**

    definition: age 15 and over can read and write

    total population: 96.3%

    male: 96.5%

    female: 95.4% (2010 est.)

**School life expectancy (primary to tertiary education):**

    total: 12 years

    male: 11 years

    female: 14 years (2009)

**Unemployment, youth ages 15-24:**

    total: 1.6%

    country comparison to the world: 129

    male: 0.7%

    female: 7.5% (2007)

# Chapter 4: Government

**Country name:**

 conventional long form: State of Qatar

 conventional short form: Qatar

 local long form: Dawlat Qatar

 local short form: Qatar

 note: closest approximation of the native pronunciation falls between cutter and gutter, but not like guitar

**Government type:**

 emirate

**Capital:**

 name: Doha

 geographic coordinates: 25 17 N, 51 32 E

 time difference: UTC+3 (8 hours ahead of Washington, DC during Standard Time)

**Administrative divisions:**

 7 municipalities (baladiyat, singular - baladiyah); Ad Dawhah, Al Khawr wa adh Dhakhirah, Al Wakrah, Ar Rayyan, Ash Shamal, Az Za'ayin, Umm Salal

**Independence:**

 3 September 1971 (from the UK)

**National holiday:**

 Independence Day, 3 September (1971); also observed is National Day, 18 December (1878) (anniversary of Al Thani family accession to the throne)

**Constitution:**

ratified by public referendum 29 April 2003; endorsed by the Amir 8 June 2004, effective 9 June 2005

**Legal system:**

mixed legal system of civil law and Islamic law (in family and personal matters)

**International law organization participation:**

has not submitted an ICJ jurisdiction declaration; non-party state to the ICCt

**Suffrage:**

18 years of age; universal

**Executive branch:**

chief of state: Amir HAMAD bin Khalifa Al Thani (since 27 June 1995); Heir Apparent TAMIM bin Hamad bin Khalifa Al Thani, fourth son of the amir (selected Heir Apparent by the amir on 5 August 2003); note - Amir HAMAD also holds the positions of Minister of Defense and Commander-in-Chief of the Armed Forces

head of government: Prime Minister HAMAD bin Jasim bin Jabir Al Thani (since 3 April 2007); Deputy Prime Minister Ahmad bin Abdallah al-MAHMUD (since 20 September 2011)

cabinet: Council of Ministers appointed by the amir

elections: the position of amir is hereditary

**Legislative branch:**

unicameral Advisory Council or Majlis al-Shura (45 seats; 15 members appointed; 30 members to be elected by popular vote beginning mid- or late 2013, per the 2003 constitutional referendum) note: the Advisory Council has limited legislative authority to draft and approve laws, but the amir has final say on all matters; Qatar's first legislative elections will be held in 2013 in which the public would elect 30 members and the Amir would appoint 15; the Advisory Council would have authority to approve the national budget, hold ministers accountable through no-confidence votes, and propose legislation; Qatar in May 2011 held nationwide elections for the 29-member Central Municipal Council (CMC) - first elected in 1999 - which has limited consultative authority aimed at improving municipal services

**Judicial branch:**

Courts of First Instance, Appeal, and Cassation; an Administrative Court and a Constitutional Court were established in 2007; note - all judges are appointed by Amiri Decree based on the recommendation of the Supreme Judiciary Council for renewable three-year terms

**Political parties and leaders:**

**Political pressure groups and leaders:**

**International organization participation:**

ABEDA, AFESD, AMF, CAEU, CD, CICA (observer), EITI (implementing country), FAO, G-77, GCC, IAEA, IBRD, ICAO, ICC (national committees), ICRM, IDA, IDB, IFAD, IFC, IFRCS, IHO, ILO, IMF, IMO, IMSO, Interpol, IOC, IOM (observer), IPU, ISO, ITSO, ITU, LAS, MIGA, NAM, OAPEC, OAS (observer), OIC, OPCW, OPEC, PCA, UN, UNCTAD, UNESCO, UNIDO, UNIFIL, UNWTO, UPU, WCO, WHO, WIPO, WMO, WTO

**Diplomatic representation in the US:**

> chief of mission: Ambassador Muhammad bin Abdallah bin Mitib al-RUMAYHI
>
> chancery: 2555 M Street NW, Washington, DC 20037
>
> telephone: [1] (202) 274-1600 and 274-1603
>
> FAX: [1] (202) 237-0061
>
> consulate(s) general: Houston

**Diplomatic representation from the US:**

> chief of mission: Ambassador Susan L. ZIADEH
>
> embassy: Al-Luqta District, 22 February Road, Doha
>
> mailing address: P. O. Box 2399, Doha
>
> telephone: [974] 488 4161
>
> FAX: [974] 488 4150

**Key Leaders:**

| Amir | HAMAD bin Khalifa Al Thani |
|---|---|
| Prime Min. | HAMAD bin Jasim bin Jabir Al Thani |
| Dep. Prime Min. | Ahmad bin Abdallah al-MAHMUD |
| Min. of Business & Commerce | JASIM bin Abd al-Aziz bin Jasim Al Thani |
| Min. of Culture & Heritage | Hamad bin Abd al-Aziz al-KAWARI |
| Min. of Defense | HAMAD bin Khalifa Al Thani |
| Min. of Education | SAAD bin Ibrahim al-Mahmud |
| Min. of Endowments & Islamic Affairs | Ghayth bin Mubarak al-KUWARI |
| Min. of Energy & Industry | Muhammad Salih al-SADA |
| Min. of Environment | Abdallah bin Mubarak al-MUDADI |

| | |
|---|---|
| Min. of Finance & Economy | **Yusif Husayn al-KAMAL** |
| Min. of Foreign Affairs | **HAMAD bin Jasim bin Jabir Al Thani** |
| Min. of Interior | **ABDALLAH bin Khalid Al Thani** |
| Min. of Justice | **Hasan bin Abdallah al-GHANIM** |
| Min. of Labor (Acting) | **Nasir al-HUMAYDI** |
| Min. of Municipal Affairs & Agriculture | **ABD AL-RAHMAN bin Khalifa bin Abd al-Aziz Al Thani** |
| Min. of Public Health | **Abdallah bin Khalid al-QAHTANI** |
| Min. of Social Affairs | **Nasir al-HUMAYDI** |
| Min. of State | **HAMAD bin Abdallah bin Muhammad Al Thani** |
| Min. of State | **HAMAD bin Suhaym Al Thani** |
| Min. of State for Cabinet Affairs | **Ahmad bin Abdallah al-MAHMUD** |
| Min. of State for Foreign Affairs | **Khalid bin Muhammad al-ATIYAH** |
| Min. of State for Interior | **ABDALLAH bin Nasir bin Khalifa Al Thani** |
| Governor, Qatar Central Bank | **ABDALLAH bin Saud Al Thani** |
| Ambassador to the US | **Muhammad bin Abdallah bin Mitib al-RUMAYHI** |
| Permanent Representative to the UN, New York | **MISHAL bin Hamad bin Muhammad Al Thani** |

**Flag description:**

maroon with a broad white serrated band (nine white points) on the hoist side; maroon represents the blood shed in Qatari wars, white stands for peace; the nine-pointed serrated edge signifies Qatar as the ninth member of the "reconciled emirates" in the wake of the Qatari-British treaty of 1916

note: the other eight emirates are the seven that compose the UAE and Bahrain; according to some sources, the dominant color was formerly red, but this darkened to maroon upon exposure to the sun and the new shade was eventually adopted

**National anthem:**

name: "Al-Salam Al-Amiri" (The Peace for the Anthem)

lyrics/music: Sheikh MUBARAK bin Saif al-Thani/Abdul Aziz Nasser OBAIDAN

note: adopted 1996; the anthem was first performed that year at a meeting of the Gulf Cooperative Council hosted by Qatar

# Chapter 5: Economy

**Economy - overview:**

Qatar has prospered in the last several years with continued high real GDP growth. Throughout the financial crisis Qatari authorities sought to protect the local banking sector with direct investments into domestic banks. GDP had rebounded in 2010 largely due to the increase in oil prices, and 2011's growth was supported by Qatar's investment in expanding its gas sector. GDP slowed to 6.3% in 2012 as Qatar's gas sector expansion moved toward completion. Economic policy is focused on developing Qatar's nonassociated natural gas reserves and increasing private and foreign investment in non-energy sectors, but oil and gas still account for more than 50% of GDP, roughly 85% of export earnings, and 70% of government revenues. Oil and gas have made Qatar the world's highest per-capita income country and the country with the lowest unemployment. Proved oil reserves in excess of 25 billion barrels should enable continued output at current levels for 57 years. Qatar's proved reserves of natural gas exceed 25 trillion cubic meters, more than 13% of the world total and third largest in the world. Qatar's successful 2022 world cup bid will likely accelerate large-scale infrastructure projects such as Qatar's metro system and the Qatar-Bahrain causeway.

**GDP (purchasing power parity):**

$189 billion (2012 est.)

country comparison to the world: 58

$177.8 billion (2011 est.)

$155.8 billion (2010 est.)

**GDP (official exchange rate):**

$184.6 billion (2012 est.)

**GDP - real growth rate:**

6.3% (2012 est.)

country comparison to the world: 34

14.1% (2011 est.)

16.7% (2010 est.)

**GDP - per capita (PPP):**

$102,800 (2012 est.)

country comparison to the world: 1

$100,600 (2011 est.)

$91,600 (2010 est.)

note: data are in 2012 US dollars

**GDP - composition by sector:**

agriculture: 0.1%

industry: 77.8%

services: 22.1% (2012 est.)

**Labor force:**

1.338 million (2012 est.)

country comparison to the world: 133

**Unemployment rate:**

0.5% (2012 est.)

country comparison to the world: 2

0.4% (2011 est.)

**Population below poverty line:**

NA%

**Household income or consumption by percentage share:**

lowest 10%: 1.3%

highest 10%: 35.9% (2007)

## Investment (gross fixed):

28.2% of GDP (2012 est.)

country comparison to the world: 28

## Budget:

revenues: $62.66 billion

expenditures: $51.19 billion (2012 est.)

## Taxes and other revenues:

33.9% of GDP (2012 est.)

country comparison to the world: 76

## Budget surplus (+) or deficit (-):

6.2% of GDP (2012 est.)

country comparison to the world: 11

## Public debt:

32.5% of GDP (2012 est.)

country comparison to the world: 108

34% of GDP (2011 est.)

## Inflation rate (consumer prices):

1.9% (2012 est.)

country comparison to the world: 26

1.9% (2011 est.)

## Central bank discount rate:

3.5% (31 December 2010 est.)

country comparison to the world: 65

5.5% (31 December 2009 est.)

## Commercial bank prime lending rate:

5% (31 December 2012 est.)

country comparison to the world: 161

4.6% (31 December 2011 est.)

**Stock of narrow money:**

$26.47 billion (31 December 2012 est.)

country comparison to the world: 63

$22.49 billion (31 December 2011 est.)

**Stock of broad money:**

$97.97 billion (31 December 2012 est.)

country comparison to the world: 55

$85.16 billion (31 December 2011 est.)

**Stock of domestic credit:**

$140.9 billion (31 December 2012 est.)

country comparison to the world: 47

$121.5 billion (31 December 2011 est.)

**Market value of publicly traded shares:**

$125.4 billion (31 December 2011)

country comparison to the world: 38

$123.6 billion (31 December 2010)

$87.86 billion (31 December 2009)

**Agriculture - products:**

fruits, vegetables; poultry, dairy products, beef; fish

**Industries:**

liquefied natural gas, crude oil production and refining, ammonia, fertilizers, petrochemicals, steel reinforcing bars, cement, commercial ship repair

**Industrial production growth rate:**

27.1% (2010 est.)

country comparison to the world: 1

**Current account balance:**

$58.57 billion (2012 est.)

country comparison to the world: 10

$51.98 billion (2011 est.)

**Exports:**

$117.7 billion (2012 est.)

country comparison to the world: 34

$114.3 billion (2011 est.)

**Exports - commodities:**

liquefied natural gas (LNG), petroleum products, fertilizers, steel

**Exports - partners:**

Japan 25.7%, South Korea 17.7%, India 9.6%, Singapore 6.3%, UK 6.2% (2011)

**Imports:**

$23.49 billion (2012 est.)

country comparison to the world: 72

$26.93 billion (2011 est.)

**Imports - commodities:**

machinery and transport equipment, food, chemicals

**Imports - partners:**

US 12.7%, UAE 12.3%, Saudi Arabia 9.3%, UK 6.2%, China 5.4%, Germany 5.2%, Japan 4.6%, France 4.6%, Italy 4.5% (2011)

**Reserves of foreign exchange and gold:**

$25.97 billion (31 December 2012 est.)

country comparison to the world: 53

$16.82 billion (31 December 2011 est.)

**Debt - external:**

$137 billion (31 December 2012 est.)

country comparison to the world: 35

$125.6 billion (31 December 2011 est.)

**Stock of direct foreign investment - at home:**

$43.83 billion (31 December 2012 est.)

country comparison to the world: 58

$38.6 billion (31 December 2011 est.)

**Stock of direct foreign investment - abroad:**

$37.34 billion (31 December 2012 est.)

country comparison to the world: 39

$31.56 billion (31 December 2011 est.)

**Exchange rates:**

Qatari rials (QAR) per US dollar -

3.64 (2012 est.)

3.64 (2011 est.)

3.64 (2010 est.)

3.64 (2009)

3.64 (2008)

**Fiscal year:**

1 April - 31 March

# Chapter 6: Energy

**Electricity - production:**

>22.28 billion kWh (2010 est.)

>country comparison to the world: 69

**Electricity - consumption:**

>17.33 billion kWh (2009 est.)

>country comparison to the world: 72

**Electricity - exports:**

>0 kWh (2010 est.)

>country comparison to the world: 120

**Electricity - imports:**

>0 kWh (2010 est.)

>country comparison to the world: 123

**Electricity - installed generating capacity:**

>3.893 million kW (2009 est.)

>country comparison to the world: 80

**Electricity - from fossil fuels:**

>100% of total installed capacity (2009 est.)

>country comparison to the world: 33

**Electricity - from nuclear fuels:**

>0% of total installed capacity (2009 est.)

>country comparison to the world: 165

**Electricity - from hydroelectric plants:**

>0% of total installed capacity (2009 est.)

>country comparison to the world: 192

**Electricity - from other renewable sources:**

>0% of total installed capacity (2009 est.)

country comparison to the world: 177

**Crude oil - production:**

1.631 million bbl/day (2011 est.)

country comparison to the world: 19

**Crude oil - exports:**

704,300 bbl/day (2009 est.)

country comparison to the world: 18

**Crude oil - imports:**

0 bbl/day (2009 est.)

country comparison to the world: 113

**Crude oil - proved reserves:**

25.57 billion bbl (1 January 2012 est.)

country comparison to the world: 14

**Refined petroleum products - production:**

153,800 bbl/day (2008 est.)

country comparison to the world: 66

**Refined petroleum products - consumption:**

169,900 bbl/day (2011 est.)

country comparison to the world: 64

**Refined petroleum products - exports:**

53,230 bbl/day (2008 est.)

country comparison to the world: 56

**Refined petroleum products - imports:**

11,940 bbl/day (2008 est.)

country comparison to the world: 129

**Natural gas - production:**

116.7 billion cu m (2010 est.)

country comparison to the world: 7

**Natural gas - consumption:**

21.8 billion cu m (2010 est.)

country comparison to the world: 36

**Natural gas - exports:**

94.9 billion cu m (2010 est.)

country comparison to the world: 4

**Natural gas - imports:**

0 cu m (2010 est.)

country comparison to the world: 121

**Natural gas - proved reserves:**

25.2 trillion cu m (1 January 2012 est.)

country comparison to the world: 4

**Carbon dioxide emissions from consumption of energy:**

64.68 million Mt (2010 est.)

country comparison to the world: 52

# Chapter 7: Communications

**Telephones - main lines in use:**

> 306,700 (2011)
>
> country comparison to the world: 114

**Telephones - mobile cellular:**

> 2.302 million (2011)
>
> country comparison to the world: 135

**Telephone system:**

> general assessment: modern system centered in Doha
>
> domestic: combined fixed and mobile-cellular telephone
> subscribership exceeds 130 telephones per 100 persons
>
> international: country code - 974; landing point for the Fiber-Optic
> Link Around the Globe (FLAG) submarine cable network that
> provides links to Asia, Middle East, Europe, and the US;
> tropospheric scatter to Bahrain; microwave radio relay to Saudi
> Arabia and the UAE; satellite earth stations - 2 Intelsat (1 Atlantic
> Ocean and 1 Indian Ocean) and 1 Arabsat

**Broadcast media:**

> TV and radio broadcast media are state controlled; home of the
> satellite TV channel Al-Jazeera, which was originally owned and
> financed by the Qatari Government; Al-Jazeera claims editorial
> independence in broadcasting; transmissions of several
> international broadcasters are accessible on FM in Doha (2007)

**Internet country code:**

> .qa

**Internet hosts:**

> 897 (2012)

country comparison to the world: 173

**Internet users:**

563,800 (2009)

country comparison to the world: 117

# Chapter 8: Transportation

**Airports:**

6 (2012)

country comparison to the world: 171

**Airports - with paved runways:**

total: 4

over 3,047 m: 3

1,524 to 2,437 m: 1 (2012)

**Airports - with unpaved runways:**

total: 2

914 to 1,523 m: 1

under 914 m: 1 (2012)

**Heliports:**

1 (2012)

**Pipelines:**

condensate 145 km; condensate/gas 132 km; gas 980 km; liquid petroleum gas 90 km; oil 382 km (2010)

**Roadways:**

total: 7,790 km (2006)

country comparison to the world: 143

**Merchant marine:**

total: 28

country comparison to the world: 87

by type: bulk carrier 3, chemical tanker 2, container 13, liquefied gas 6, petroleum tanker 4

foreign-owned: 6 (Kuwait 6)

registered in other countries: 35 (Liberia 5, Marshall Islands 29, Panama 1) (2010)

**Ports and terminals:**

Doha, Mesaieed (Umaieed), Ra's Laffan

# Chapter 9: Military

**Military branches:**

      Qatari Emiri Land Force (QELF), Qatari Emiri Navy (QEN),

      Qatari Emiri Air Force (QEAF) (2012)

**Military service age and obligation:**

      18 years of age for voluntary military service; no conscription

(2010)

**Manpower available for military service:**

      males age 16-49: 389,487

      females age 16-49: 165,572 (2010 est.)

**Manpower fit for military service:**

      males age 16-49: 321,974

      females age 16-49: 140,176 (2010 est.)

**Manpower reaching militarily significant age annually:**

      male: 6,429

      female: 5,162 (2010 est.)

**Military expenditures:**

      10% of GDP (2005 est.)

      country comparison to the world: 2

# Other Key Facts™ Titles

Key Facts on Syria

Key Facts on China

Key Facts on Qatar

Key Facts on India

Key Facts on Germany

Key Facts on Argentina

Key Facts on Russia

Key Facts on North Korea

Key Facts on Brazil

Key Facts on Italy

Key Facts on the United Arab Emirates

Key Facts on the European Union

Key Facts on Pakistan

Key Facts on Saudi Arabia

Key Facts on Cyprus

Key Facts on Iran

Key Facts on Afghanistan

Key Facts on Iraq

Key Facts on Indonesia

Key Facts on South Korea

All Key Facts™ Titles are Available at

www.Amazon.com

# THE INTERNATIONALIST®

# 2013

www.internationalist.com

www.ingramcontent.com/pod-product-compliance
Lightning Source LLC
Chambersburg PA
CBHW051418170526
45165CB00004BA/1871